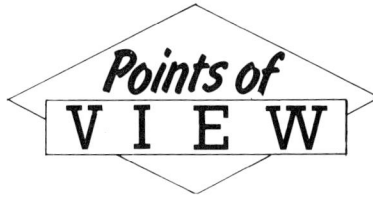

*Points of*
# VIEW

# ·D·R·U·G·S·

## Christian Wolmar

Wayland

# Points of View

Abortion
Advertising
Alcohol
Animal Rights
Apartheid
Capital Punishment
Censorship
Divorce

Drugs
Medical Ethics
Northern Ireland
Nuclear Weapons
Racism
Sex and Sexuality
Smoking
Terrorism

**Front cover:** *An initiate smokes a pipe of crack. A derivative of cocaine, crack is extremely addictive. In the USA, crack use has become established in almost every inner city.*

**Editor:** William Wharfe
**Consultant:** Andrew Fraser, Director of the Drug Advice and Information Service (DAIS).
**Designer:** David Armitage

First published in 1990 by
Wayland (Publishers) Limited
61 Western Road, Hove
East Sussex BN3 IJD, England

**British Library Cataloguing in Publication Data**
Wolmar, Christian
    Drugs – (Points of view)
    1. Drug abuse
    I. Title II. Series
    362.2'93

ISBN 1-85210-649-2

Phototypeset by Direct Image Photosetting Limited,
Hove, East Sussex, England
Printed in Italy by G. Canale & C.S.p.A., Turin
Bound in France by A.G.M.

# Contents

# 1 Introduction

> The word drug encompasses far more than just the chemicals used by addicts and the medicines we take when we are ill. It actually means any substance which has an effect on the body . . . It includes things we eat, things we drink, things we smoke, even things we breathe. (Jenny Bryan, *Drugs for All?* 1986.)

> A drug can be considered any substance other than food which by its chemical nature affects the structure or function of a living organism. (National Commission, *Drug Use in America*.)

The use of drugs is almost as old as humankind. Cave dwellers probably picked plants for both medicinal and recreational purposes. Yet, as can be seen from the two quotations above, it is very hard to define exactly what a drug is.

**Left** *The Greeks were the first to discover wine, which was made in the same way as today — by allowing grapes to ferment.*

There are an estimated 4,000 plants which can alter people's moods when taken and about 60 have been in consistent use throughout history; tea, coffee, alcohol, cannabis, opium and coca are some of them. As for medical drugs, we know that in Egypt by 1500 BC, there was a list of 700 drugs taken to cure ailments. Some, such as opium and saffron, are still in use today. We know too, that in classical Greece and Rome, alcohol was already widely drunk and some scholars of the time mention the problems of alcohol abuse.

Each culture had its own drugs. Cocaine was taken by Incas in South America and had a central role in their religious and social systems throughout their civilization, which stretched from around AD 1200 to AD 1550. Coffee roasting developed in Arabia in the fourteenth century. As Europeans travelled the world in the sixteenth century, they brought back a host of new drugs – coca, cocoa, the kola nut and tea.

Many drugs that we routinely use today were once prohibited and illegal. Coffee was banned in the Ottoman Empire, but with little success. In the seventeenth century, in parts of Germany and Russia, the penalty for smoking tobacco was death. In the USA, alcohol was banned from 1920 to 1933.

*Opium dens were once legal in many parts of Asia, but have now been outlawed.*

5

*When these three men (Middleton, Price and Koet) became the first to smoke tobacco publicly, in London during the sixteenth century, they were regarded as objects of curiosity.*

However, many drugs that are now strictly controlled and illegal were once freely available. In the UK, in the early nineteenth century, opium could be bought over the counter without a prescription from chemists and even grocers. Cocaine and cannabis were both legal until the early twentieth century in both the UK and the USA.

Various societies over the ages have also had widely differing definitions of when consumption of a drug becomes 'drug abuse'. Even severe drunkenness was considered acceptable behaviour at the time of James I of England. While everybody would probably agree that the drug addict who is damaging his or her health by injecting dangerous substances every day is a 'drug abuser', what of the person smoking 60 cigarettes per day or the office worker who gets drunk every Friday night? Here is one typical definition of drug abuse.

> Drug abuse is behaviour, as designated by professional and other community representatives, describing the use of particular drugs in particular ways for particular reasons which are contrary to the agreed upon rituals in a given community at a given point in time. (National Commission, *Drug Use in America*).

Most books on drugs focus solely on drugs or substances taken for pleasure or habit. While this book, too, concentrates on these 'recreational' drugs, it also briefly examines medical drugs. This is because it is simplistic and misleading to draw an absolute dividing line between the two. For example, barbiturates are prescribed by doctors for their sedative effect. But they are also taken by people without medical supervision to get 'high'. Even heroin, the drug most associated with addiction and the problems involved with it, has a medical use as a painkiller. In the UK, it is already widely used as such, but in the USA there has been strong resistance:

> Heroin, a scourge of America's inner cities, is also an extremely effective painkiller that many physicians believe could help desperately ill cancer patients. That is why two [US senators] are leading an uphill fight to allow treatment of terminal cancer victims with the drug. . . Some physicians argue that equally effective narcotics are currently available. . . Some law enforcement officials fear that this legal heroin will escape to the street market. Neither argument stands scrutiny. No physician would be forced to prescribe heroin . . . and the amount stockpiled . . . would be too small to make much difference in the street supply if some were to leak out. (*New York Times*, 14 January 1988.)

This book also covers both legal drugs such as alcohol and tobacco, and illegal drugs such as cannabis and heroin. This is because the issues raised by the use of these drugs are the same.

The UK government recognized this when, just after Christmas 1988, it launched a campaign which sought to tackle both the problems of drug and alcohol abuse. No one knows the extent of illegal drug use:

> It is impossible to tell accurately how many people take illegal drugs in Britain because it is an activity that takes place in secret. All the available statistics rely on drug abusers coming to the attention of the authorities and no one knows what proportion these are of the total number. It is thought that several million people have taken cannabis, with about a million taking the drug in a year. Amphetamines are the next most popular drug, although they come a long way behind cannabis. Cocaine use has increased sharply but its expense has limited its appeal. It is heroin use and addiction that has increased most since the mid-seventies. Studies in London and Newcastle during the 1980s suggest that the true number of addicts may be five times the number notified to the Home Office (about 15,000 in 1987). (*New Society*, 22 January 1988.)

This book makes no attempt to cover all the commonly used drugs, legal or illegal, but uses a selection of drugs to raise particular issues of interest to the reader.

1  How do you define a drug?

2  What is the difference between a drug taken for medicinal purposes and recreational purposes?

3  At what point does drug use become drug abuse?

4  Why is it so hard to find out how many people use illegal drugs?

*Although thousands of people are arrested for drugs offences each year, they represent only a tiny proportion of users.*

# 2

# Why drugs are used and how they work

Remarkably little is known about the way many drugs work. Manufacturers and doctors merely know that the drugs they produce and prescribe are useful in helping sick people and do not have any dangerous side effects.

Most drugs work either by boosting levels of chemicals in the body that are too low or by reducing the level of those that have become too high. More commonly, they do the latter. Others, like vaccines, are designed to make the body produce chemicals to help fend off attacks from illnesses.

The paths travelled by drugs through your body are complicated. Some are aimed at particular organs, others affect all parts of the body through the central nervous system. Alcohol, for example, is a 'depressant', which means that it slows you down. It is absorbed through the stomach and small intestine into the bloodstream. Once in the blood, alcohol travels to all areas of the body quite quickly, affecting the working of the brain. The depressant effect of alcohol means that signals sent out by your brain take longer to reach their destination. Reaction times are slowed down, which is why it is so dangerous to drink and drive.

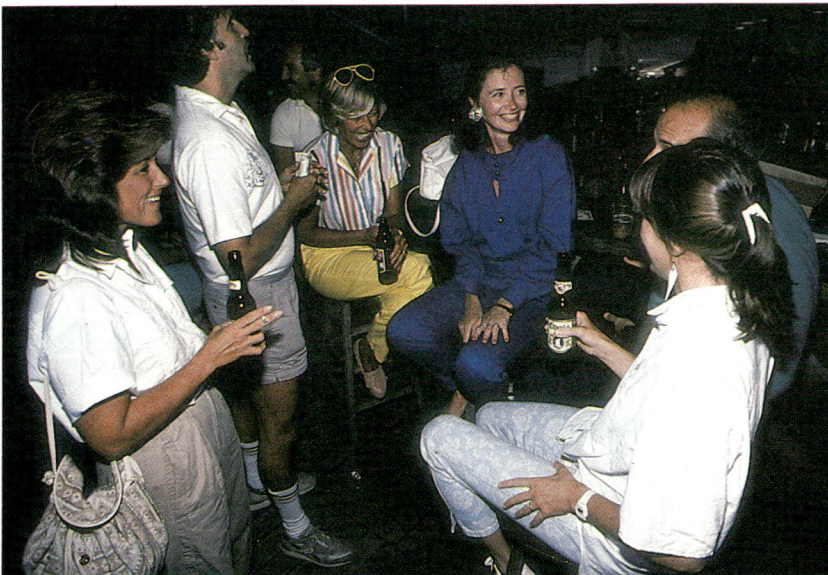

*Perfectly legal — as long as the drinkers are not under age and do not drive home after having too many.*

One of the least understood ways that drugs work is the 'placebo' effect. Placebo drugs are dummy pills given to a patient which work because the patient *thinks* they will work. There is no medical or chemical explanation for their effect, but it has been documented by many scientists.

> Placebos belong to that twilight world of medical science that has never quite been able to claim respectability. This is a pity because the placebo effect is both interesting and important. It is important in practical terms because it is a major therapeutic influence in many medical treatments. It is important in theoretical terms because it highlights the psychological component of the response to drugs. (Michael Gossop, *Living with Drugs*, 1982.)

In the UK around £2 billion of the National Health Service's cash is spent each year on various tablets, pills, ointments and other drugs. Two-thirds of patients leaving the surgery come out clutching a prescription for some sort of medicine.

*In addition to prescribed drugs, home remedies are big business as this scene from a cough linctus factory shows.*

> No one knows how often drugs work or fail but many, possibly most, drug treatments do not benefit patients at all . . . Over 200,000 tablets were collected by chemists during a three week 'amnesty' in Dudley, Hereford and Worcester [in Britain]. Three years later, in a similar exercise, 300,000 were collected. And an astonishing 740,000 tablets were collected during the amnesty in 1982. (Charles Medawar, *The Wrong Kind of Medicine*, 1984.)

However, other nations consume much more. While the average British citizen collects six or seven prescriptions from the doctor each year, in France and Italy the figure is ten and in the USA between sixteen and seventeen.

That is not to say that all drugs are useless or only work through the placebo effect. Far from it. A person suffering from diabetes who does not get their insulin will simply die. Even some types of cancer can be beaten with the use of powerful drugs, and the effects of the AIDS virus can be reduced by drugs, even though no drug has so far been found which kills the AIDS virus itself.

*1   Why do you think the placebo effect works?*

*2   Why are so many medicinal drugs left unused?*

*3   Why do you think some countries consume more medicinal drugs than others?*

*The effects of the hallucinatory drug LSD (lysergic acid diethylamide) or 'acid', are highlighted in the 1967 film* The Trip, *starring Peter Fonda (pictured here). LSD first became widely used in the USA in the 1960s — a person taking the drug is said to be 'on a trip'.*

# 3

## Illegal drugs

> Today there are four big recreational drugs on the market of most of the world's big cities. Two of them (alcohol and tobacco) are legal, two (marijuana and cocaine) illegal. People have been attacking their brains with the first of these poisonous chemicals since Noah had vines. Christianity uses alcohol in its central rite, as does most of mankind (outside the strict Muslim nations) in its social relations. Yet in countries like Britain, lawful alcohol directly kills some 10,000 people a year and is instrumental in about half of the country's violent crime. Cigarettes in Britain kill 100,000 a year. Marijuana, one of the illegals, has hardly killed anybody. (*The Economist*, 2 April 1988.)

Assuming there are 50,000 heroin addicts with a habit costing around £50 a day to buy the drugs; if only half of them have to live by stealing to maintain their habit, then over £6 million-worth of goods are stolen by addicts every day.

### ● Cannabis

Cannabis is one of the most commonly used recreational drugs. It comes in several forms, all derived from the cannabis plant, mainly as dried leaves or as resin which seeps out from parts of the plant. It is usually smoked in pipes or as 'joints' mixed in with tobacco, but the leaves can be smoked on their own.

**Below** *Cannabis is the most widely used illegal drug in both Europe and North America.*

In 1987, UK customs officers seized 16,277 kg of cannabis, 358 kg of cocaine and 295 kg of heroin.

Cannabis is reckoned by most scientists to be the least harmful of the illegal drugs:

> Cannabis is not addictive; it produces little tolerance, that is, regular users do not have to increase the amount to achieve the same effect, and it does not cause any hangovers. There are no reported cases of death from cannabis overdose and compared to other drugs it has an extremely low toxicity. The quantity of cannabis necessary to produce a lethal dose is so large that only a rough estimate can be made at about 1.5 lbs [0.7 kg] eaten in one go. (Release Drug Education Series, *Cannabis*.)

Yet, cannabis is by far the cause of the most prosecutions, for drugs offences, by the police. Nearly 20,000 people in the UK are dealt with by the courts for cannabis offences each year, the vast majority for possession of small amounts of the drug. This has led to successive campaigns to have cannabis legalized.

*Many farmers in the developing countries, like this Colombian peasant growing cannabis, are economically dependent on exporting crops for illegal drug use.*

Opponents of the legalization of cannabis argue that long-term, regular, and heavy cannabis smoking may, like tobacco smoking, help cause diseases such as bronchitis or lung cancer. They point to the danger created by intoxication under the influence of cannabis; the drug taker will not be able to drive or cross roads as safely as when they are not under the drug's influence; its use can lead to other drugs:

> It was during the 1960s that marijuana became the drug of revolt, smoked by millions of young people as a symbol of their escape from the petty tyrannies of bourgeois [middle-class] behaviour. It became regarded as a harmless drug which could be used to heighten the pleasure of parties, rock concerts and other enjoyable activities. Its proponents have often exaggerated the harmlessness of marijuana, just as its critics once overstated its ill-effects. For while it is true that marijuana is less habit-forming than heroin or cocaine, it can lead to dependency and it can provide a 'bridge' to other, more powerful, drugs. (The Observer Modern Studies Handbook, *Drugs*.)

Supporters of legalization say that it would free police for more productive activities and improve community relations, since cannabis use is thought to be particularly prevalent among the Afro-Caribbean population in the UK:

> The outright legalization of marijuana would be the single most effective move towards restoring the rule of law in our cities. (Ian Aitken, *The Guardian*.)

**Above** *Many people believe that legalizing 'soft' drugs like cannabis would make the drive against 'hard' drugs like heroin easier.*

The number of people found guilty of drugs offences in 1986 in the UK was: cannabis 19,049, amphetamines 2626, heroin 2232, cocaine 446; others 1449.

## ● Cocaine

Cocaine is a stimulant derived from the coca leaf grown in South America and taken as white powder, usually sniffed through the nose. Like cannabis, cocaine only became illegal in the USA and the UK in the twentieth century. It was originally an ingredient of Coca Cola, but now the drink is made using 'decocainized' coca leaves. It used to be very expensive and was therefore dubbed the 'yuppy drug' because it is taken by many rich and famous people. It has recently become cheaper.

The drug's effect is to make people more alert, keep them awake, and generally stimulate them. Many people have been attracted to cocaine because it is not physically addictive – that is, there are no withdrawal symptoms. However, users can become psychologically dependent on it because it makes them confident, cheerful and energetic. Long-term constant use is damaging to health in a number of ways. The membranes lining the nostrils can become damaged, stomach complaints can develop and heart problems may result. If taken in large doses or over prolonged periods it can cause heart attacks. In the USA, the death of two sports stars in 1986 put the spotlight on the dangers of cocaine.

**Above** In 1986, basketball star Len Bias (right) died from a heart attack after using cocaine. The death shocked the USA; he had been the most promising player of his generation.

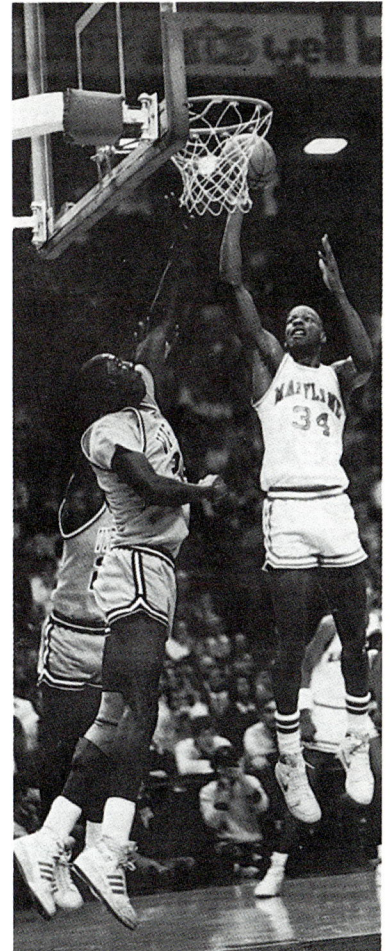

**Left** The pressures of high-powered jobs and the high salaries that go with them tempt many into using expensive drugs like cocaine.

15

Because cocaine is so highly priced and is aimed at higher income groups, the smuggling trade in the drug has become astonishingly lucrative. In August 1989 the USA sent $69 million of aid to Colombia in an attempt to crush the powerful drug barons.

> The Latin American drugs trade is reckoned to be worth as much as $110,000 million a year. Indeed, leaders of the Medellin Cartel, the biggest drug ring, are reported recently to have offered to settle Colombia's foreign debt in exchange for an amnesty. (*Daily Telegraph*, 1 March 1988.)

Crack, derived from cocaine, is smoked, usually from a pipe. The 'high' that the user experiences is usually more intense than that experienced with cocaine. Crack is highly addictive, and if taken regularly can cause serious heart problems. However, the drug is so new that it is not yet possible to know what the drug does to someone who takes it over a long period. It first appeared in large quantities in the USA in 1988, and the effects of the drug have been felt most strongly in Washington DC. In 1988, largely because of drug-related crime, Washington DC overtook Detroit as the most violent city in the USA. Behind that crime rate is the sudden, overwhelming demand for the drug.

**Above** *While cocaine in Western countries is sniffed as a white powder, it is very widely used in South America in its raw form as coca leaves which are chewed. They can be seen here in Bolivia — as easy to buy as the potatoes next to them.*

> ... The murders tell only part of the story. The Drug Enforcement Administration (DEA) has calculated that the citizens of the Greater Washington area are now spending $24 million a day on cocaine [and hence crack]. This amounts to $8 billion a year, almost as large as the US space budget and substantially more than the three million inhabitants spend on eating and drinking. (John Lichfield and Marc Champion, the *Independent*, 24 July 1989.)

## ● Heroin – and other opiates

The type of heroin available in the UK is mixed with similar looking powders – or 'cut' to reduce its purity – and sold to drug users. It can be dissolved in water and injected, sniffed like cocaine, or smoked. Recently, 'chasing the dragon' has become a popular way of using it. This involves heating heroin and breathing in the fumes, often through a small tube.

While the newspapers have exaggerated and distorted the risks, heroin is undoubtedly a very dangerous drug. People are attracted by the feelings of contentment and warmth the drug gives them. There can be immediate unpleasant effects such as being sick or feeling nauseous, but these tend to disappear.

**Below** *Drugs seized by the authorities are destroyed like these 9 tonnes of cocaine being burnt in Mexico, but much more slips through the net.*

CAMPAÑA
ERMANENTE

CONTRA EL
NARCOTRAFIC

14.NOV.88

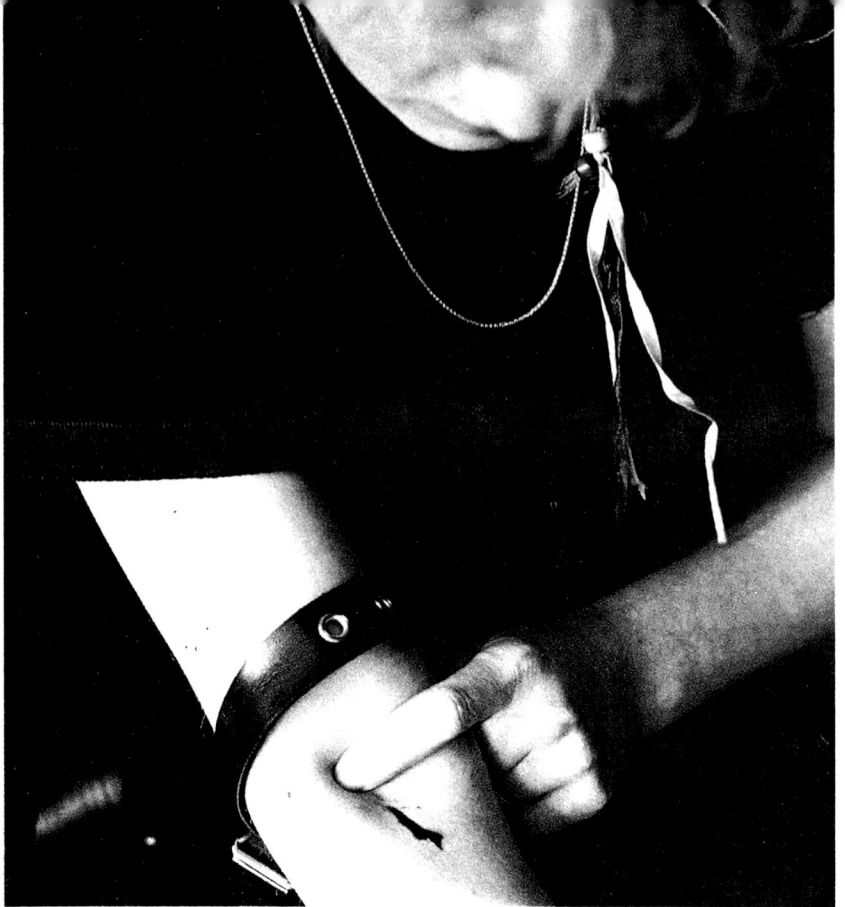

*A heroin addict after injecting. Regular injections can damage the area where the needle is inserted. If the needle is not sterile the user risks infection.*

The great danger of heroin is that it is strongly addictive. Although at first addiction is purely psychological, as with cocaine, gradually it becomes a physical addiction. In other words, if a person stops using the drug, there are real physical withdrawal symptoms, a feeling likened to a bad bout of flu. Many addicts say, however, it feels much worse than any flu they ever had.

Misleading media stories can be very harmful:

> One story, emanating from Cheshire, had pushers creeping about in school playgrounds injecting cartons of milk with heroin, thus causing one shot addiction and a queue of customers. One clear element in this total picture is racism; the moral panic over pushers of heroin and other illegal intoxicants carries with it a popular assumption that pushers are foreigners and aliens. (*Drug Use and Misuse; a Reader,* 1987.)

The popular media has spread a false message by suggesting that one shot of heroin is enough to get you hooked for life. This hinders the work of those trying to stop or limit the use of the drug. People using the drug for the first time will discover that it is not immediately addictive, certainly not an immediate killer, but will then go on to ignore much more sensible advice about the risks from drugs agencies, doctors and others. The media tends to portray 'the drugs pusher' as an evil influence who preys on young people. In fact, most people obtain their first drugs from a friend and again they become confused between their own experience and the impression created by the media.

The question of how to treat the growing number of addicts has become an increasing source of controversy. Because AIDS can be spread through shared needles and many people who inject drugs are not careful about hygiene, the issue has become one of increasing urgency. Because of fears about the spread of AIDS, the British government began to offer practical and realistic advice to drug injecters on how to clean their syringes. It also set up 'needle exchange' schemes where old needles could be swapped for new clean ones.

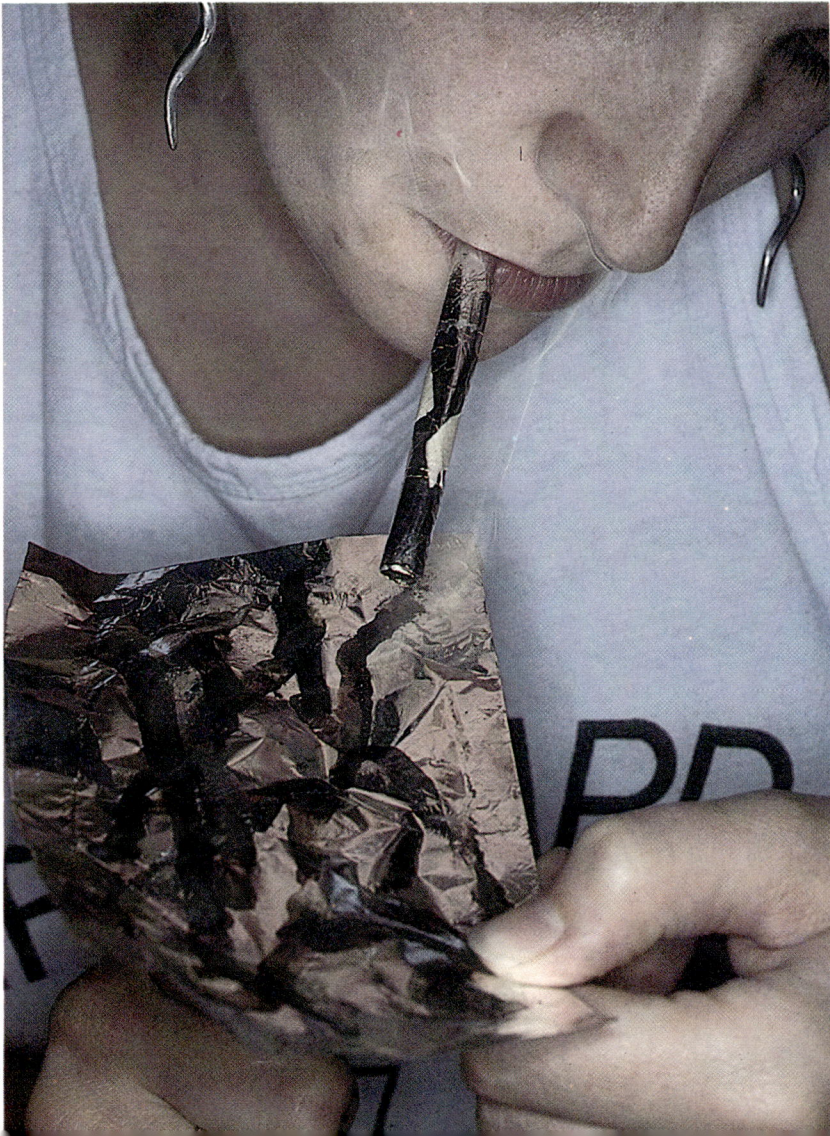

*Heroin can be smoked as well as injected.*

*The enormous increase in drugs misuse in the USA has led to an assortment of drugs prevention campaigns, including 'Just say no to drugs', aimed at teenagers. It was initiated in 1986 by Nancy Reagan, who was First Lady of the USA at the time.*

In the USA, drug problems have become so widespread, that politicians and commentators increasingly compare the situation to a war:

> Drugs are killing this country [the USA], street by street, victim by victim. A feeling of helpless despair has come over the country. President and Mrs Reagan preach the message of 'Just say no' from the White House and insist that the corner has been turned. The statistics show otherwise. One in six American adults is now a drug user. Drug posses [gangs] have pushed urban violence to an all time record. Only a mile from the White House, pregnant women and six-year-old children are being shot dead, families 'executed' in a wave of murderous rivalry among pushers. People are being killed in the nation's capital at the rate of almost one a day, 67 per cent of them the victims of drugs wars. (Michael Binyon, 'Washington View', *The Times*, 12 March 1988. © *Times* Newspapers Limited 1988.)

**Above** *A sickening experience — heroin addicts in Thailand are made to vomit, after taking a herbal medicine to help their cure from addiction.*

Getting people off drugs, therefore, has not just become a matter of helping these individuals but of protecting society.

In the UK, there has been a unique system of treatment since 1968 when a series of special clinics, called Drug Dependency Units (DDUs), were established across the country. Originally, the idea was to allow addicts to be supplied with drugs legally, but often they were given a heroin substitute called methadone in the form of a syrup so that it could not be injected. However, this idea of 'maintaining' the addicts' habit gradually lost favour and now the units tend to try to reduce the addicts' doses over a period of six to twelve weeks.

> The Drug Dependency Units did not continue this policy [of maintenance]. During the 1970s, attitudes changed and many doctors decided that maintenance was not a satisfactory approach. To many doctors, maintenance seemed to be a policy of hopelessness. It confirmed in the minds of many addicts that they could not do without drugs, so denying them any hope of coming off. Addicts often sold some of the drugs which they were being prescribed, which helped the drugs habit to spread. (The Observer Modern Studies Handbook, *Drugs.*)

DDUs are often unsuccessful. One recent study showed that of 138 people referred to an Edinburgh clinic, less than half turned up and only four were drug-free six months after their referral. This poor record is leading the units to reassess their work and their role. For instance, the use of methadone has been widely criticized:

> The touting of one drug as cure for dependence on another is a recurring theme in pharmacological history. For those hooked on opium, the far stronger morphine was once advanced. For morphine addicts, cocaine and then heroin was pushed. For overcoming heroin addiction, methadone [another potent addictive drug] is currently being dispensed by the State. What is true about all these classes of drugs is that problems rapidly accumulate when the leap is made from the comparatively mild substance found in nature to the synthesized, streamlined product of the laboratory. (Andrew Tyler, *Street Drugs*, 1988.)

*The shared use of needles by drug addicts is one of the main ways of spreading AIDS and has led to education campaigns by many Western governments.*

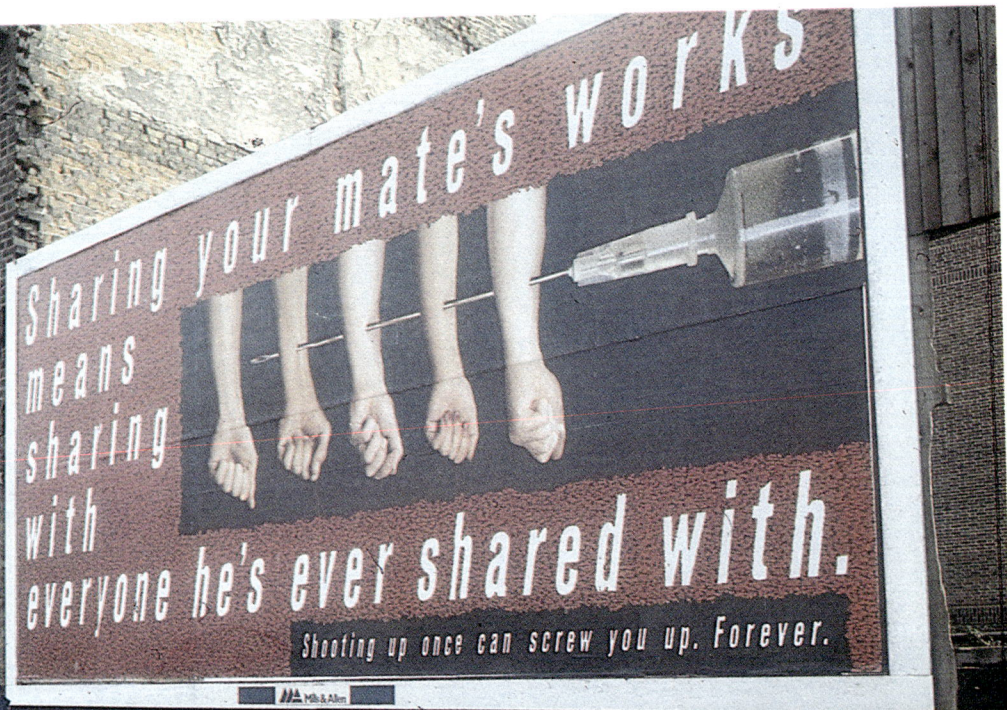

● **Decriminalization**

Drug use has increased dramatically over the past ten years, despite anti-drugs campaigns and higher penalties against drug dealers and users. There is a widespread recognition that existing measures have been ineffective even though the penalties are increasingly harsh:

> The large quantities of heroin and cocaine seized by HM Customs and Excise have had no effect on price and purity. This indicates a plentiful supply. Further, the continuing low price and continuing high purity level has happened at a time when the demand has increased rapidly. It can only be concluded that the supply of hard drugs is more than matching the market. (Society of Civil and Public Servants, 1985.)

*The Bulldog Café in Amsterdam, one of the few cities in the world where cannabis in small quantities can be bought legally over the counter.*

23

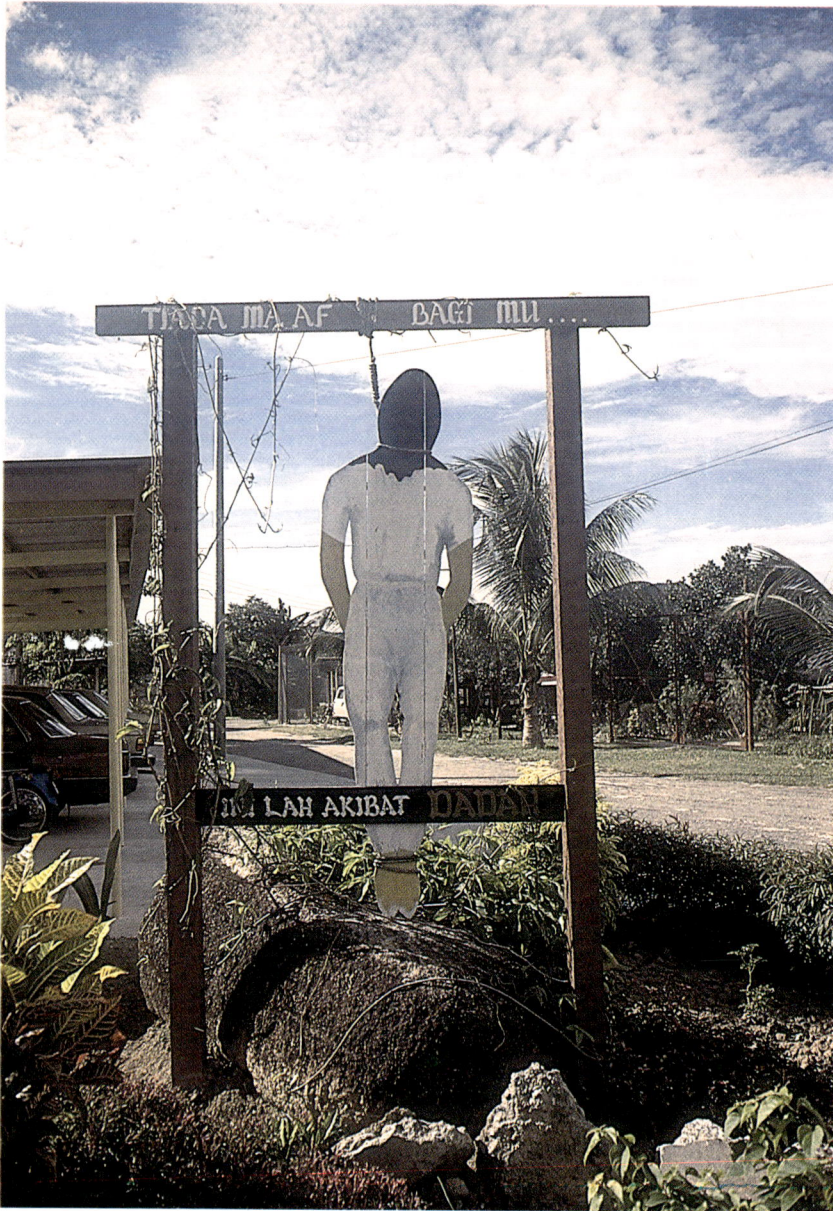

*Malaysia. A powerful reminder to drug offenders of the fate that awaits dealers. Several Westerners, including Briton Derrick Gregory in July 1989, have been hanged as a result of the law which means an automatic death penalty for all drugs smugglers who are caught in Malaysia.*

Because of this failure of existing policies, there is growing support for a very radical solution – decriminalizing drugs. In the early 1980s, the Standing Conference on Drug Abuse (SCODA), a leading organization in the drugs field, supported a move to make legal the personal use of a small quantity of any drug. Now many respectable and famous figures are supporting a similar move, partly because AIDS can be spread through sharing needles to inject drugs. If drugs are made legal, then fewer people would be forced to share needles. A series of articles has begun appearing in conservative newspapers in the UK, such as the *Daily Mail*, the *Sunday Telegraph* and *The Economist,* suggesting different ways of taking the law out of the drugs issue:

> If it were no crime to take drugs, the price would fall and crimes would fall with it. This does not imply approval. The Government has extended drinking hours but it does not approve of alcoholism. If drug use were decriminalized, it would in fact be easier to tackle the ill-effects they can cause, including the contamination by AIDS which spreads to non-users. (Paul Barker, *Sunday Telegraph*, 15 May 1988.)

> The best policy towards existing heroin users might be to bring them within the law, allowing them to register for the right to buy strictly limited doses. Taxes should be high enough to help deter consumption but low enough to put illicit [unlawful] dealers out of business. To get addicted to heroin, you have to be crazy or weak willed or young and foolish. It is a problem of mental health, treated as one of crime and therefore made worse. If some extra stick is wanted, then in America registered heroin and cocaine users could be disqualified from driving cars. They might then have an incentive to get listed as cured. (*The Economist*, 2 April 1988.)

**But the British government has so far stuck to its position:**

> This Government has always given the highest priority to tackling drug misuse and will continue to do so. What we will not do is to decriminalize drugs, as has been suggested recently by a small but vociferous minority not only in the US but in this country as well.
>
> Critics who liken our policy on drugs to the prohibition of alcohol in the US during the Twenties are making a false analogy. Prohibition was abandoned when it ceased to command public support. Even today, the number of Americans who seriously consider that drugs such as heroin or cocaine should be freely available is very small indeed. (Douglas Hogg, UK Home Office Minister, 1988.)

It will be interesting to see, over the coming years, which methods in different countries prove most effective in dealing with the problem of drug addiction. Some of the drugs listed in this chapter may one day be legalized, while for other drugs the punishments for drug dealing may become harsher and the police work more intensive and sophisticated.

*Most politicians, like Britain's Douglas Hogg (pictured here), are still opposed to legalizing drugs, but a growing minority are beginning to support a radical change in the laws. In 1988, in the UK, the British Society for Normalization of Drug Laws was established.*

*1 Why do you think that some drugs are legal and others illegal?*

*2 Do you think there would be more or fewer drug addicts if heroin were made legal? Do you think there would be more or fewer alcoholics if alcohol were made illegal?*

*3 What do you think a poor country like Colombia can do about its drugs industry?*

# 4

## Legal drugs

### ● Alcohol

> Alcohol is the world's most widely abused drug. Its abuse at present undermines British law and order far more than marijuana or cocaine. The typical Briton is seen abroad as a drunk wrapped in a Union Jack. We tempt young people to the point of destruction with lavish drink advertising, lax licensing laws, a hands-off approach to irresponsible publicans, cheap alcohol and no random breath tests. Consumption is soaring. One third of 15-year-olds are now considered 'regular nightly drinkers'. Alcoholism is by far the greatest threat to children's health and safety, more than smoking and certainly more than drugs. (Simon Jenkins, *Sunday Times*, 29 May 1988.)

Alcohol is the most obvious example of a harmful drug that is legal. It comes in many forms, from beer with as little as 3 per cent alcohol to spirits like vodka which can have as much as 50 per cent.

Alcohol is a very powerful drug which gives drinkers a feeling of being relaxed and can make people more talkative. The danger of alcohol is partly recognized by governments in that they place restrictions on who can buy it and the hours pubs and restaurants can sell it. It is against the law in the UK for anyone under eighteen to buy or drink alcohol in a pub. In the USA (except in Wyoming), people have to be over 21 before they can buy alcohol.

> Between 500,000 and 850,000 people in England and Wales have a serious drink problem.

**Below** *Champagne has a very glamorous image. However, though it may cost ten times more than beer, the morning-after headache feels just the same.*

**Above** *Driving whilst drunk is the biggest single cause of death on the roads.*

In 1988, the British government extended licensing laws in England and Wales to allow pubs to remain open in the afternoon and for an extra hour on Sundays. This move was fiercely opposed by some groups concerned about alcoholism who felt it would increase drunkenness and who point to a wide range of social problems caused by alcohol:

> Between 20 per cent and 70 per cent of murderers have been drinking prior to committing the offence; between 20–30 per cent of violent offences occur in or near pubs; more than 50 per cent of men who batter their partners are regularly drunk; 40 per cent of male prisoners and 25 per cent of female prisoners are said to drink at levels dangerous to their health. (UK Home Office report.)

The opponents of liberalization said that it was contradictory for the British government to announce, almost simultaneously, a crack down on young 'lager louts'. They also pointed to the experience of Scotland after the licensing laws were relaxed in 1977.

> Contrary to popular belief, alcohol consumption in Scotland *did* go up as a result of the changes [more liberal pub opening hours introduced in early 1977] – by 13 per cent between 1976 and 1984 – and would have gone up even more but for rising unemployment. Since the changes, deaths from cirrhosis of the liver in Scotland have gone up by a third, half as much again as in England and Wales. (Alcohol Concern.)

As with other legal drugs like tobacco and tranquillizers, there is a very powerful lobby run by the manufacturers who put pressure on politicians to relax the drinking laws further. There have been strong criticisms of the way young people are shown in advertisements for alcoholic drinks. Drinks manufacturers currently operate a voluntary code which says that people who look under 25 will not be portrayed in advertisements.

Islamic societies ban alcohol entirely and it was prohibited in the USA between 1920 and 1933, a period called the Prohibition.

> The growth of the Prohibition movement and the failure of national Prohibition have greatly affected the American response to drug use and to all subsequent attempts at its control. To many, Prohibition is an example of the futility of restrictive legislation against any drug use; others lament that a reaction to a unique and unfortunate experience has since prevented the development of any effective program for the control of alcohol use. (US Department of Housing, Education and Welfare, *Perspectives on the History of Psychoactive Substance Use.*)

The Prohibition experiment was a dramatic failure because it did not have whole-hearted public support and because illegally produced and imported drink was widely available. It is, therefore, very unlikely to be repeated again in a Western society.

One argument often used by drinks manufacturers is that a little drinking is good for you. Indeed, one famous slogan, used intermittently for over 50 years, is that 'Guinness is good for you'. This was based on the research showing that moderate drinkers tend to be healthier than both heavy drinkers and teetotallers,

**Above** *Rum being destroyed during the Prohibition in the USA; one of the great failed social experiments of the twentieth century.*

Three people die every day in the UK because of drunken drivers. That's more than are murdered.

people who abstain completely. In fact, the reason why teetotallers tend to be less healthy is that many are former drinkers who have had to give up completely because of the damage to their health or are people who have medical complaints like diabetes which makes it inadvisable to take alcohol. So, in fact, there is no convincing evidence that alcohol consumption is good for people.

● **Glues, solvents and gases**

Although often called 'glue-sniffing', there are a number of commonly used substances apart from glue which can be inhaled or sniffed. It has been calculated that at least 30 products in the average home can be abused by a 'sniffer'.

During the Prohibition in the USA, over 280,000 illegal distilleries were seized by the police in 1930 alone.

*Allowing pubs to remain open for longer each day resulted in increased drinking in Scotland after the law was changed in 1977.*

Between 1980 and 1986, 530 young people died in the UK from sniffing solvents. Of these, 167 had been sniffing gas fuels, 90 had sniffed aerosols, 145 had sniffed glue and 178 had sniffed other substances.

While in the USA 'sniffing' became established in the 1950s, in the UK it is a relatively recent phenomenon. It started in the 1970s, and there is still widespread ignorance about the best ways of tackling the problem.

Like alcohol, glue and other solvents have a sedative effect, but the experience is much shorter lived, about half an hour, and often includes dream-like hallucinations. Reactions to the products can vary enormously, depending on the individual and his or her mood.

Sniffing is almost entirely confined to teenagers, the peak ages being twelve to sixteen. It is a cheap alternative to alcohol and is usually done in groups.

About 100 young people die each year in the UK from solvent abuse. Because of concern about these tragedies, a law was passed in 1985 making it an offence for shopkeepers to supply solvents if they had reason to suspect that the product would be inhaled.

The problem for those trying to enforce the law is that many young people want to buy these products for perfectly legitimate reasons and often retailers are only prosecuted after a tragedy has been caused:

>   Among the first [to be convicted under the Intoxicating Substances (Supply) Act 1985] was a Southwark newsagent convicted of supplying four or five bottles of Tipp-Ex thinner to a local 14-year-old. The boy died after sniffing with his friends in a local park. The newsagent received three months imprisonment. (Andrew Tyler, *Street Drugs*, 1987.)

*Sniffing directly from a bottle is a dangerous way of inhaling solvent. Solvent abuse kills over 100 young people in the UK every year.*

30

# Killers on the shelves

By John Burns

EVERY six days a child dies in Britain as a direct result of the craze for sniffing solvents.

That is the official figur.e Police and social workers are convinced the true death toll is far higher.

And the terrifying fact is that most of these young victims will not have bought their glue, lighter fuel or whatever under-the-counter from some shady back-street trader.

Most of them will have made their purchase openly, from the shelves of a perfectly respectable High Street store.

The cashier will probably have wrapped the tube or can in a polythene bag, unwittingly providing an instant sniffing kit.

**THE VICTIMS**

For the bleak truth is that

*Extra research by* DAVID JACK, MICHAEL CHARLESTON, DAVID WOODING, JOHN KING, ALAN BAXTER and JOHN LEY.

and they promised further action to t ry to ensure staff kept to them.

IN WORCESTER a volunteer 12 - year - old bought

Brown said the shops' reaction was encouraging, but fell well short of what was needed.

The greatest problem was that more than 300 items were used by solvent abuses.

IN ROCHDALE, Lancashire, two teenage girls bought a pint of glue at

WE RESERVE THE RIGHT TO REFUSE SALES OF GLUE TO PERSONS UNDER 18 YEARS OLD 'THE BEST WAY TO DO IT... B&Q IT!'

Youths at a glue stand. Above, warning notices. *Picture :* VICTOR BLACKMAN

## Region where one in five youngsters are hooked

There have been suggestions about introducing a law to force glue manufacturers to add foul smelling substances to their products, but this was rejected by the British government because of fears that it would be counter-productive:

> It seems fortunate that glue additives have not been used in this country [Britain], particularly in view of the American experience that actions taken solely to prevent glue-sniffing cause the abusers to turn to other available substances such as aerosols or butane, the abuse of which seems to be more dangerous and leads to an increase in the number of deaths. It would seem that sniffing glue, rather than other substances, is the least dangerous form of inhalant misuse. (Joyce Watson, *Solvent Abuse, the Adolescent Epidemic*, 1985.)

It is often not the solvent sniffing itself which proves fatal but the circumstances around it. Following the first media scare stories in the early 1960s, researchers in the USA found that among tens of thousands of glue sniffers, no death was due solely to the glue vapour. The life-saving advice children needed, they concluded, was not to sniff glue with their heads in plastic bags.

*The new law which makes it a crime for shopkeepers to sell glue and other solvents to young people if they know that it will be used for sniffing, is very hard for the police to enforce. It is often only used after there has been a tragedy.*

Much of the health education material has recognized that since many children are bound to try glue-sniffing, the most important thing is to ensure they do it safely:

> Don't sniff in dangerous places, such as balconies, busy roads, canal and river banks. Solvents are quick to affect the body.
> Don't sniff alone, as there will be no one around to help in case there's an accident.
> Don't put glue directly on your face or mouth or you may suffocate yourself.
> Don't use a large bag or polythene bag. If there is any chance of the bag going over your head, or becoming stuck to your nose or mouth, you run the risk of suffocation.
> Don't mix glue with other drugs, especially alcohol.
> (Release, *Sniffing Glue and Other Solvents*, 1981.)

There used to be much more concern about the long-term dangers of glue-sniffing, but this is now played down: most children only ever try it a few times and evidence of long-term damage has been greatly exaggerated:

> No one suggests that sniffing isn't dangerous. However, it need not be as dangerous as is commonly assumed. Health educators are particularly worried at how the media portray the subject, often concentrating on individual youngsters whose lives are a horrifying mess, implying that this is because of sniffing, ignoring the possibility that the sniffing may reflect a much deeper psychological problem. One reassuring point is that despite stories in the media about permanent damage to the brain, kidneys or other organs caused by long-term sniffing, such damage is in fact extremely rare. (Institute for the Study of Drug Dependence, *Drugs, what every parent should know,* 1988.)

Since it seems likely that most of the products used by 'sniffers' are going to continue to be easily available in the shops, anyone who is thinking of 'sniffing' should at least pay attention to advice such as that on page 32. Otherwise they may risk serious injury or even death.

A survey of 3000 pupils at six London comprehensive schools revealed that 12 per cent had tried cannabis, 11 per cent had sniffed solvents, and just under 2 per cent had tried heroin.

*Prevention is the best form of cure, as here with drugs education in the classroom.*

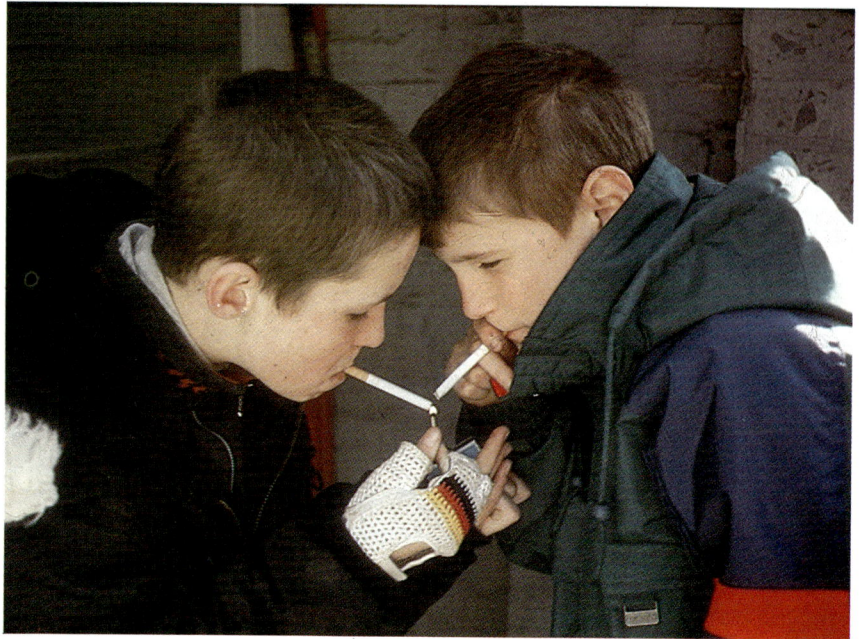

*While older people are smoking less because they have become aware of its dangers, young people are ignoring these warnings and continuing to take up the habit.*

● **Tobacco**

Each year, British people smoke just under 100 billion cigarettes. No one quite knows why smoking is so attractive or why people become addicted. Some research suggests that the most active ingredient, nicotine, can both stimulate and depress the central nervous system, depending on the person's mood and the amount of the drug being consumed. Other research discounts the importance of nicotine.

What is certain is that smoking kills. The health dangers of tobacco have been very well documented and, according to doctors, smoking causes the deaths of 100,000 people per year in the UK from lung cancer and other respiratory and heart diseases. This terrible toll has been likened to other epidemics which were caused by government failure to take action:

> At a time when some 100,000 of our citizens are dying prematurely from [smoking's] effects every year and millions more die elsewhere, the Royal College of Physicians would be failing in its duty if it did not urge the government to reverse its present attitude of inactivity and even of encouragement towards the tobacco industry and tackle this hidden holocaust with the urgency once given to cholera, diphtheria, poliomyelitis and tuberculosis. (British Royal College of Physicians, *Health or Smoking*, 1983.)

On average, out of 1000 young male adults in England and Wales who smoke cigarettes, one will be murdered, six will be killed on the roads and 250 will be killed prematurely by tobacco.

However, apart from banning the sale of tobacco to people under the age of sixteen, the British government imposes few restrictions on smoking. Cigarette – though not cigar – advertising is banned on television, but the government has resisted attempts to stop all advertising. The government's dilemma is that revenue from taxes on tobacco – around £1 per packet of 20 – is its third largest source of revenue, worth almost £6,000 million annually:

> Smoking is primarily a health problem, although it does play a significant economic role in the community. While cigarette tax is a rich source of revenue to the Treasury, the costs of smoking to the economy include not only the cost of treating diseases caused by smoking, but also other costs such as working days lost and social security payments. (Action on Smoking and Health (ASH) factsheet.)

A Japanese survey has suggested that non-smoking wives of men who smoke 20 or more cigarettes a day are twice as likely to develop lung cancer as non-smoking wives married to non-smoking men.

*As smoking decreases in the West, the tobacco companies are targeting developing countries for their promotion campaigns.*

# No wonder smokers cough.

**The tar and discharge that collects in the lungs of an average smoker.**

The Health Education Council

*The money spent on campaigns against smoking is a tiny proportion of the advertising budget of the big tobacco firms.*

However, tax revenue far outweighs the cost to the British National Health Service of treating diseases caused by smoking, which is reckoned to be £500 million per year. Some cynics point out that the premature deaths caused by smoking save the government money in pensions which would otherwise have to be paid to old age pensioners.

One area that is attracting increasing attention is 'passive smoking', the effect on the health of non-smokers of other people smoking near them.

> Companies which allow unrestricted smoking on their premises risk prosecution because of a more aggressive stance by local councils' environmental health officers. The new approach has been adopted as a result of a government sponsored report which said that inhaling other people's smoke was associated with an increased risk of lung cancer in non-smokers. (The *Observer*, 4 September 1988.)

The issue of passive smoking makes it much more difficult for the tobacco industry to defend itself. In 1979, the major companies started funding a pressure group called FOREST which has consistently argued that the freedom to smoke is a fundamental civil right. However, if passive smoking increases the risk to people who choose not to smoke, then the issue is not so simple.

There has been a steady decline in smoking since the early seventies, in response to fears about the health dangers, although in 1988 there was a small increase in the UK. The tobacco industry has responded by looking for new markets. Special cigarettes

*Many more restaurants, cinemas and shops now ban smoking as the link between inhaling other people's cigarette smoke and cancer has been proved. But in many places, non-smokers still have to put up with other people's smoke.*

*If smoking continues to decline in the West, many farmers in developing countries, like these Zimbabwean tobacco growers will have to find alternative crops.*

aimed at women have been introduced and smoking among women actually rose in 1988. New products which you chew rather than smoke have been developed. The inhabitants of the developing world, who are less likely to be informed of the health dangers of smoking, have also been targeted:

> Why, given their immense problems of poverty and disease, do Third World governments allow the burden of smoking to be peddled to their people? Bribed by big tax revenues, governments are conned into believing that tobacco is good for them — a good cash crop for the farmers, a product which the people want, a commodity which the country can export.

In fact cultivator, consumer and country are getting a uniquely raw deal. The farmers, hooked by the help and advice which the tobacco companies lavish on them, end up growing a crop which takes more labour than any other for diminishing returns. The smoker is callously, if not criminally, being sold cigarettes packing twice the punch of cancer-causing tars as that of the rich world's cigarettes. The international brand names are the same but there are seldom health warnings on the wrapper. (Mike Muller, *Tomorrow's epidemic,* 1978.)

*1 Do you think there should be more or fewer restrictions on the drinking of alcohol?*

*2 Do you think that young people are more likely or less likely to try glue sniffing if they have read a leaflet advising them on 'sniffing' safely?*

*3 In 1988, cigarette smoking went up in the UK by 2 per cent, the first rise for 20 years. Can you give some possible reasons for this increase?*

*4 Do you think poor countries should grow tobacco? Give reasons both for and against the idea.*

# 5

# Medical drugs

There are probably over 5,000 different drugs in use to treat diseases and illness. While many of these are clearly useful, there is growing concern about the overuse of drugs. The British National Health Service spends some £2 billion on drugs each year. Some are simply useless, others have bad side effects and others prove to be addictive:

> People who use legal drugs obtained by prescription often develop dependency in the same way as people who use illegal drugs, abuse alcohol or smoke cigarettes. Unlike other forms of drugs use, addiction to prescription medication results from drug use introduced by a physician. (Sharon Zalewski, 'Prescription Drug Addicts: Reflection of Social Ills,' *Engage/Social Action*, July/August 1985.)

There is also considerable waste as can be seen by looking at the contents of the average bathroom cabinet which is stacked full of unused drugs.

**Below** *Controls over drugs are much more lax in many poor countries and many dangerous drugs can be bought without a doctor's prescription as here at a chemist's in Dhaka, India.*

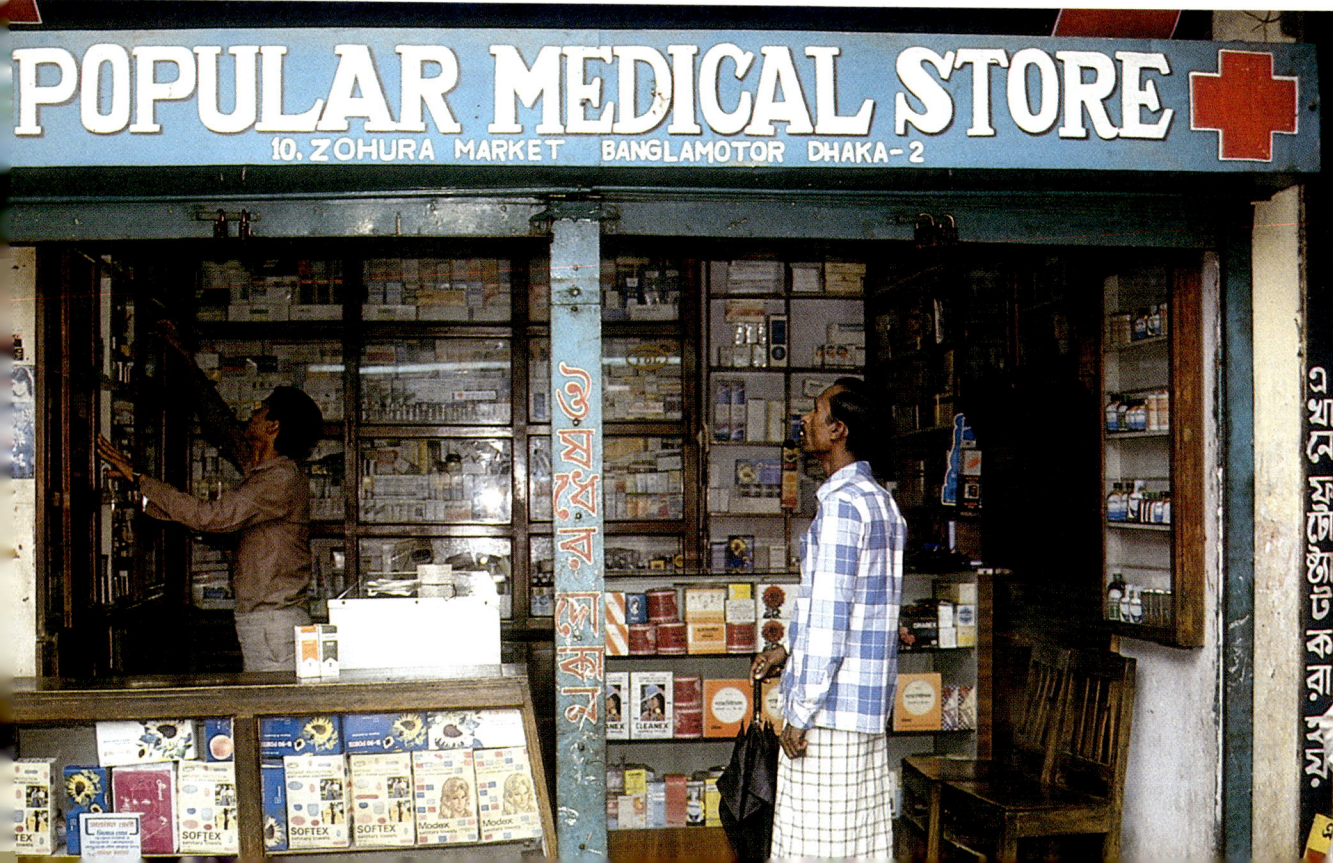

POPULAR MEDICAL STORE

10. ZOHURA MARKET   BANGLAMOTOR DHAKA-2

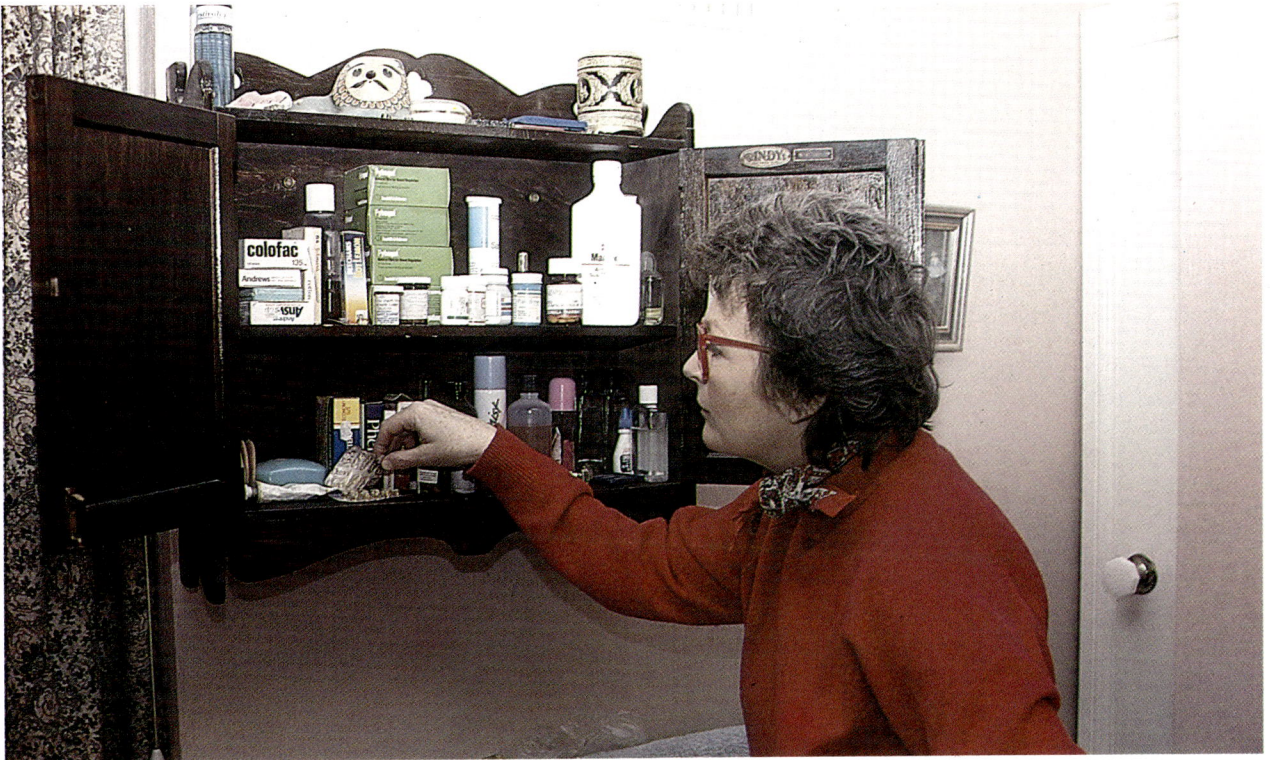

**Above** *Bathroom cabinets may end up full of unused drugs because doctors are sometimes over eager to prescribe them, but patients may be reluctant to take them.*

● **Tranquillizers**

In the early 1960s, a range of new drugs whose effect was to calm people's moods, was introduced. Officially called minor tranquillizers, or benzodiazepines, they were said not to have the same addictive effect of the stronger barbiturates which they partly replaced. In fact, they proved to be highly addictive:

> It is now difficult to talk about taking tranquillizers without the problem of dependence being mentioned. Many of those who are taking tranquillizers believe themselves to be addicted and many more who could benefit from taking them are afraid to do so in case they become addicted. Yet 15 years ago people were quite happy to take these drugs. It was even suggested that most tranquillizers were so safe that it was not necessary for doctors alone to prescribe them. (Peter Tyrer, *How to Stop Taking Tranquillizers*, 1986.)

> With tranquillizers, the physical withdrawal symptoms include: sweating, shaking, insomnia, pins and needles, jelly legs, changes in how you perceive things (e.g. daylight seeming very bright), lack of co-ordination, and lack of confidence. (Release, *Trouble with tranquillizers*, 1982.)

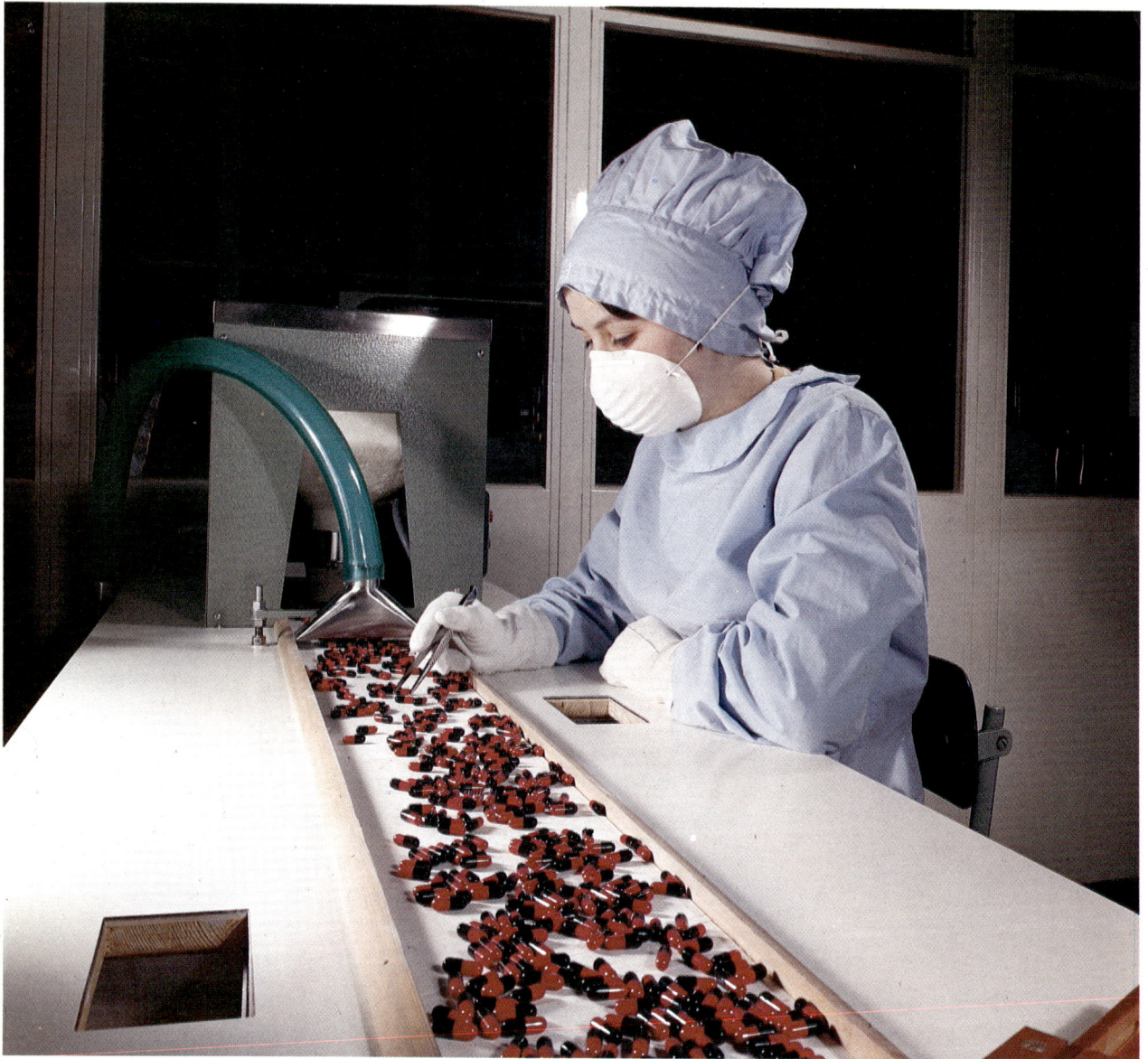

*The big pharmaceutical companies thoroughly test drugs before they are marketed, but errors still slip through. Minor tranquillizers were once thought to be harmless, but are now known to be highly addictive.*

Tranquillizers are very widely used and, therefore, the problems they cause affect a substantial proportion of the population. Doctors now tend only to prescribe them for short periods, because they recognize that after a few days or weeks, the pills lose their effectiveness. Once they have overcome the difficulties and the withdrawal symptoms, people who have stopped using tranquillizers after a long period of taking them — up to 20 years sometimes — say they have been given a new lease of life, feeling things for the first time in years and being generally happier and more cheerful.

## ● Drugs in sport

The disqualification of Ben Johnson (who finished first in the 100 m race in the 1988 Seoul Olympics) because he took anabolic steroids, put the spotlight on the use of drugs in sports. The international sports authorities ban over 4,000 substances because they are likely to enhance an athlete's performance.

The basic arguments against the use of drugs in sports is that it should be the athletes' ability and strength, not the drugs, which enable them to win. The example they set for young people and the dangers of drug use are also considered important.

> Inevitably, sport, being an integral part of society, has been caught up in the drug culture. Social, economic and national pressures are imposed on athletes to win, sometimes at any cost. Athletes, who embark upon the path of drug misuse, not only begin to destroy their own sense of moral values and of fair play, but damage their sport and the ethics of the Olympic Movement . . . Leaders, both in sport and of athletes, must do all in their power to keep drugs out of sport, making sport an example and an inspiration for young people, when all around drug misuse is causing problems. (Statement of International Olympic Committee Medical Commission.)

However, some doctors and sports commentators say that drug rules in sport should be relaxed:

> The amount of unfairness introduced by drug taking is no greater than that of runners using pacemakers or of a few athletes having access to advanced physiological and sports medicine laboratories while the majority do not. (Andrew Nicholson, Editor, *Journal of Medical Ethics*.)

A wide variety of drugs are used by certain athletes. A West German heptathlete, Birgit Dressel, died aged 26 after having over 400 injections of body-building and other drugs in a year. She had gone from being ranked twenty-sixth in the world to sixth during that time. Some athletes use stimulants to increase their heart rate, anabolic steroids to boost muscle development, beta blockers to ease anxiety, and diuretics – which stimulate urination – to flush out other drugs in their bodies.

**Above** *High jumper Birgit Dressel who died at the age of 26 from the effects of drugs she took to improve her performance.*

*1   What are the differences between being addicted to a medical drug and a recreational drug?*

*2   Should drugs like anabolic steroids be made illegal, or should athletes be allowed to use them in order to perform better?*

# 6 Conclusion

This book has raised a lot of questions over drug use and has demonstrated that there are no simple answers to many of these issues. However, there is widespread agreement that as a society we use too many drugs, both legal and illegal. Many of the effects of these drugs are harmful, but some are enjoyable and in the case of medical drugs, therapeutic. Yet overall, even in the case of medical drugs, there is a tendency to use too many and to turn to the bottle of pills before other forms of treatment are considered.

However there is less agreement on how society should try to reduce this consumption. Should doctors be encouraged to prescribe less? Should there be stricter controls on alcohol and tobacco, and stronger punishment against those using or dealing in illegal drugs? Or would it be better to reduce controls?

Apart from controls, the main way that society reacts to the use of recreational drugs is through drugs education. Because young people are regarded as being most in danger from drugs, the educational material is targeted towards them. There are two basic types of drugs education – one which stops any drug-taking whatsoever and the other which recognizes that some young people will inevitably try some drugs.

*The grassroots campaign against crack. A street 'poster' in New York City speaks for itself.*

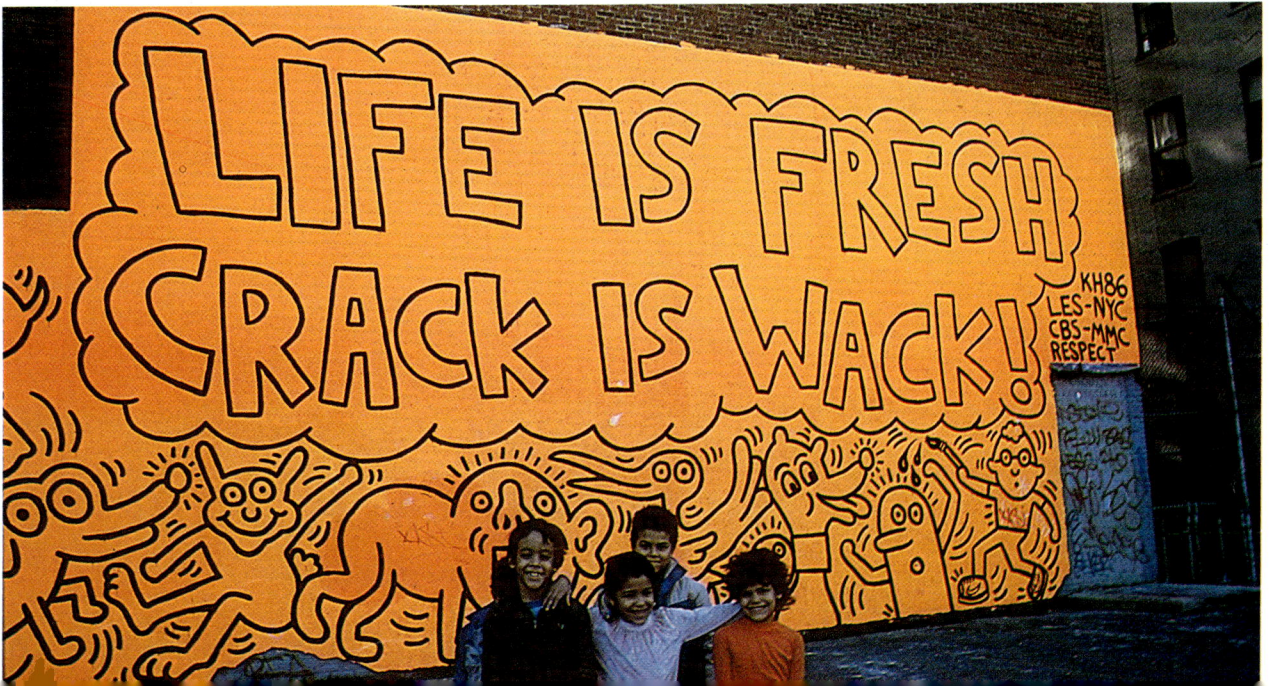

There is a bitter controversy over which one is more effective. In England the Department of Health tends to favour the 'shock horror' approach, while in Scotland the Home and Health Department has adopted 'harm-minimization' and has criticized the English 'Heroin screws you up' campaign. In the USA, President Reagan and his wife, Nancy, strongly aligned themselves with the more traditional approach and developed the idea of 'zero tolerance', meaning that the aim should be to stop all drug-taking:

> The whole problem of drug abuse was being denied. For too long, our nation has denied that a problem even existed. We denied that drug abuse had health and social consequences . . . There was almost a stigma in trying to take on drugs. It was unfashionable. It was illiberal and narrow-minded in our live-and-let-live society. Movies and television portrayed drugs as glamorous and cool . . .

I have a message for the drug dealers and producers and pushers: The parents throughout the world are going to drive you out of business. We're the ones who are going to be the pushers from now on. We're going to push you out of our schools, our neighbourhoods, our communities, and out of existence! (Nancy Reagan, Address to the World Affairs Council, Los Angeles, 24 June 1986.)

*Nancy Reagan pictured in 1986 during a publicity event for her 'Just say no to drugs' campaign. On the issue of the fight against drugs she said, 'I always thought if we could just get the young people involved it would be a giant step forward.'*

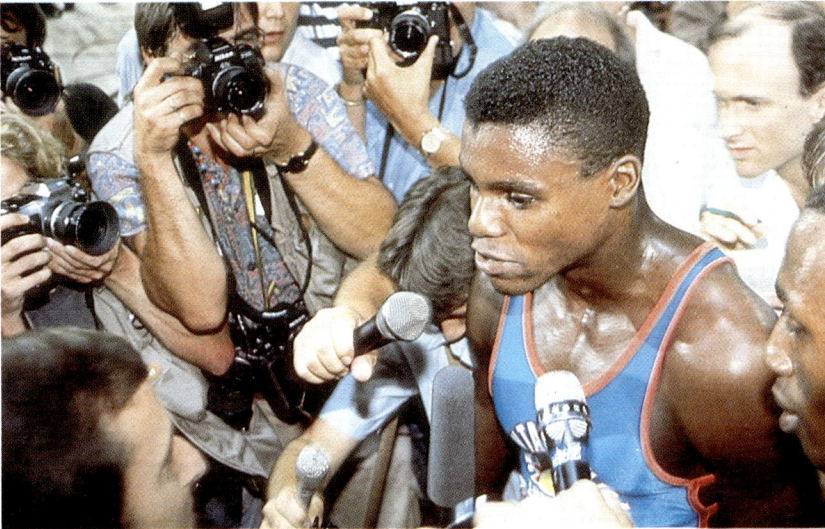

*Carl Lewis — the eventual Olympic 100 m champion at Seoul in 1988. He has fought the use of drugs in sports, and drug abuse in general, throughout his sporting career.*

There are also those who oppose any form of drugs education, arguing that it will only increase curiosity and tempt young people into trying them. Overall, however, the harm minimization approach is becoming more favoured by professionals working with drug addicts and young people:

> 'I am dismayed by the ineffectiveness of drugs education in schools, none of which has prevented the rise of a new generation of users. We have to accept that we don't know how to stop people taking drugs, but we can reduce the harm they suffer in taking them,' says Alan Parry, project director of the Drugs Training Information Centre. The biggest killer is solvent abuse. Glue was taken off the shelves when children sniffed it so they simply turned to solvents. They die because they are so ignorant about what they can and can't sniff.

Harm Minimization is not just about reducing physical side effects. The project emphasizes that you can lose your job, get into debt, be arrested and get a criminal record. It also focuses on the effects drugs can have on the family and the community as a whole. Harm Minimization sounds defeatist, but Parry is convinced it is simply realistic. 'The majority of kids come in contact with drugs. Our policies are dealing with the kids who said yes.' (Joanna Coles 'Reducing risks for children who won't say no', *Daily Telegraph*, 16 August 1988.)

Either way, one thing is certain. The problem of drugs misuse and the ethical and moral issues raised by the use of all drugs are going to be with us for a long time.

1 Which type of drugs education do you think is most effective?

2 Think of five ways to reduce drugs use.

3 Do you use, or have you ever used drugs? If you do use drugs — why do you? Are you likely to go on using drugs for some time? How difficult would it be for you to give up?

4 Is there anything that is not officially a drug which you are to some extent 'addicted' to?

# Glossary

**Addict** A person who is physically or psychologically unable to stop taking a drug.

**AIDS** Acquired Immune Deficiency Syndrome, a deadly disease often caught by drug users sharing needles to inject drugs.

**Amnesty** A period designated by the government when people can hand over illegal possessions without the fear of prosecution.

**Amphetamines** Commonly known as speed, whizz, sulphate, or uppers, a group of drugs which make people more active and energetic.

**Barbiturates** Highly addictive and commonly known as 'downers', a group of addictive drugs once widely prescribed to help people relax or sleep.

**Cannabis** A mild drug, also known as hash, blow, dope, or marijuana, obtained from the hemp plant, either in resin or leaf form and smoked, often with tobacco.

**Cirrhosis** A chronic disease of the liver which progressively kills off cells, caused by drinking too much alcohol.

**Cocaine** A drug, normally taken as a powder sniffed through the nose, which produces a short-lived effect, dulls pain and makes the user energetic.

**Cut** To reduce the strength of drugs by adding other substances.

**Decriminalization** The removal of the legal penalties attached to an illegal act, so that it can be committed without fear of punishment.

**Dependent** To be addicted.

**Depressant** A drug that slows the body down.

**Drugs ring** An illegal organization which makes a business of producing and distributing illegal drugs internationally.

**Hallucination** A false impression in the mind induced by certain types of drugs (hallucinogens).

**Heptathlon** An athletic event for women in which contestants take part in seven different track and field sports over two days.

**Heroin** A highly addictive and widely used drug which can be injected, sniffed or smoked.

**High** To be under the influence of a drug.

**Intoxication** A state of drunkenness, elation or stupor caused by taking alcohol or certain drugs.

**Joint** A cigarette containing cannabis.

**Legalization** To make something lawful.

**Licit** Lawful.

**Medicinal** For medical purposes.

**Methadone** A drug often given by clinics to heroin addicts as an alternative to heroin.

**Narcotics** A group of drugs, including heroin, which causes the user to feel numb and sleepy.

**Nauseous** Feeling on the verge of vomiting.

**Placebo** A 'dummy' pill, often just sugar, given by doctors, usually in experiments.

**Prohibition** The period in the 1920s and 1930s in the USA, when making and selling alcohol was banned.

**Proponent** A person who puts forward or supports a particular viewpoint.

**Psychological addiction** Dependence on a drug causing a change in one's mental and emotional state, rather than having a physical craving for it.

**Pusher** A person who sells illegal drugs.

**Recreational drugs** Drugs taken for fun rather than medical purposes.

**Sedative** A drug which has a soothing, calming effect.

**Shot** An injection.

**Sniffing** Taking drugs — most commonly cocaine, amphetamines, or solvents — through the nose.

**Solvents** Liquids in which other substances are dissolved, often used by 'sniffers'.

**Stimulant** A drug which boosts people's energy and makes them excitable.

**Toxicity** The extent to which a substance is poisonous.

**Tranquillizers** A group of drugs used to alleviate anxiety.

**Vociferous** Being noisy and vehement when making a protest or putting forward an argument.

**Withdrawal** Coming off a drug, often accompanied by unpleasant physical and mental symptoms.

# Further Information

Addiction Research Foundation, 33 Russell Street, Toronto, Ontario M5S 2SI, Canada.

Alcohol and Drug Foundation, PO Box 269, Woden, Australia Capital Territory, Australia 2606.

Institute for the Study of Drug Dependence, I Hatton Place, London ECIN 8ND. (Tel: 0I-430 I99I) ISDD provides information on drugs and drugs misuse, publishes various leaflets and has a library (visits by appointment).

National Clearing House for Alcohol and Drug Information, PO Box 2345, Rockville, MD 20852, USA.

Release, I69 Commercial Street, London EI 3BW. (Tel: 0I-377 5905/0I-603 8654 24 hour number) Advice on legal problems arising from drug misuse.

## Further reading

Armitage, R. *Let's Discuss Drinking* (Wayland, 1987)

*Drug Alert – The Basic Facts* (BBC, 1988) – Available from BBC Radio One, London WIA 4WW

Hawkes, N. *The International Drugs Trade* (Wayland, 1988)

Leigh, V. *Let's Discuss Drugs* (Wayland, 1986)

Leigh, V. *Let's Discuss Smoking* (Wayland, 1986)

McCall Smith, A. and E. *So you want to try drugs?* (Chambers, 1986)

Tyler, A. *Street Drugs* (New English Library, 1988)

## For teachers

Heller, T., Gott, M., Jeffrey, C. (eds) *Drug Use and Misuse: A Reader* (John Wiley, 1987)

*Drugs and Young People in Scotland: An Introduction for Teachers and Others Concerned with Young People* (Scottish Health Education Group, 1986)

# Acknowledgements

The publishers have attempted to contact all copyright holders of the quotations in this title, and apologise if there have been any oversights.

The publishers gratefully acknowledge permission from the following to reproduce extracts from copyright material: Central Independent Television, *Drugs for All*, by Jenny Bryan, 1986; Consumer's Association, *The Wrong Kind of Medicine*, 1984; Croom Helm, *Solvent Abuse, the Adolescent Epidemic*, by Joyce Watson, 1985; *The Daily Telegraph:* (I) article, I March 1988; (2) article by Paul Barker, 15 May 1988; (3) article, 'Reducing risks for children who won't say no' by Joanna Coles, 16 August 1988; *The Economist*, article, 2 April 1988; *The Guardian*, article by Ian Aitken; the *Independent*, article, 'Crack of Doom: drug that is killing a city', by John Lichfield and Marc Champion, 24 July 1989; Institute for the Study of Drug Dependence, *Drugs, what every parent should know*, 1988; New English Library, *Street Drugs* by Andrew Tyler, 1988; *New Statesman and Society*, article, 22 January, 1988; *The New York Times*, editorial 'This Heroin Fix Ought to Be the Law', 14 January 1988; *The Observer:* (I) article, 4 September 1988; (2) Observer Modern Studies Handbook, *Drugs*; Open University, *Drug Use and Misuse: A Reader* 1983; *Police Review*, article, 22 January 1988; Release: (I) *Cannabis*; (2) *Sniffing Glue and Other Solvents*, 1981; (3) *Trouble with Tranquillizers*, 1982; Royal College of Physicians, *Health or Smoking*, 1983; Sheldon Press, *How to Stop Taking Tranquillizers*, by Peter Tyrer, 1986; *The Times:* (I) article, 'Creeping Drugs Crisis Contaminates the Veins of a Nation', by Michael Binyon; (2)*Sunday Times*, article by Simon Jenkins, 29 May 1988; War On Want, *Tomorrow's epidemic*, by Mike Muller, 1978; Wildwood House, *Living with Drugs*, by Michael Gossop, 1982.

The publishers would like to thank the following for providing the illustrations in this book: All-sport (Bob Martin) 45; British Museum 4; Camera Press (Ogden Gigli) *cover*, (Brian Eads) 21; Colorsport 42; David Cumming 35; John Frost Historical Newspapers 31; Sally & Richard Greenhill 29, 33, 34; Health Education Council 36 (top); Hutchison 13; Kobal Collection II; Macdonald/Aldus Archive 28, 40; Peter Newark 5, 6; Christine Osborne 22, 23, 24, 38, 39; Edward Parker 10; Photo Co-op (Vicky White) 18, (Crispin Hughes) 30; Photri 15 (right), 20; Rex Features (David Browne) 8, 12, 26, 32, 43; Select Pictures (David Hoffman) 14, 19, (Liba Taylor) 17; South American Pictures (Tony Morrison) 16; Topham Picture Library 9, 25, 41, 44; Zefa Picture Library 15 (left), 27, 36 (bottom), 37.

# Index

Page numbers in bold refer to illustrations